CW00557083

Greater Than a Tourist
Book Series
Reviews from Readers

I think the series is wonderful and beneficial for tourists to get information before visiting the city.

-Seckin Zumbul, Izmir Turkey

I am a world traveler who has read many trip guides but this one really made a difference for me. I would call it a heartfelt creation of a local guide expert instead of just a guide.

-Susy, Isla Holbox, Mexico

New to the area like me, this is a must have!

 -Joe, Bloomington, USA

This is a good series that gets down to it when looking for things to do at your destination without having to read a novel for just a few ideas.

-Rachel, Monterey, USA

Good information to have to plan my trip to this destination.

-Pennie Farrell, Mexico

Great ideas for a port day.

-Mary Martin USA

Aptly titled, you won't just be a tourist after reading this book. You'll be greater than a tourist!

-Alan Warner, Grand Rapids, USA

Even though I only have three days to spend in San Miguel in an upcoming visit, I will use the author's suggestions to guide some of my time there. An easy read - with chapters named to guide me in directions I want to go.

-Robert Catapano, USA

Great insights from a local perspective! Useful information and a very good value!

-Sarah, USA

This series provides an in-depth experience through the eyes of a local. Reading these series will help you to travel the city in with confidence and it'll make your journey a unique one.

-Andrew Teoh, Ipoh, Malaysia

GREATER THAN A TOURIST- ANTIGUA & BARBUDA

50 Travel Tips from a Local

Dr Carolyn Edmondson

CZYK Publishing Since 2011.
CZYKPublishing.com
Greater Than a Tourist

Mill Hall, PA
All rights reserved.
ISBN: 9798839469495

>TOURIST

50 TRAVEL TIPS FROM A LOCAL

BOOK DESCRIPTION

With travel tips and culture in our guidebooks written by a local, it is never too late to visit Antigua and Barbuda. Greater Than a Tourist- Antigua and Barbuda by Author Dr Carolyn Edmondson offers the inside scoop on Antigua and Barbuda. Most travel books tell you how to travel like a tourist. Although there is nothing wrong with that, as part of the 'Greater Than a Tourist' series, this book will give you candid travel tips from someone who has lived at your next travel destination. This guide book will not tell you exact addresses or store hours but instead gives you knowledge that you may not find in other smaller print travel books. Experience cultural, culinary delights, and attractions with the guidance of a Local. Slow down and get to know the people with this invaluable guide. By the time you finish this book, you will be eager and prepared to discover new activities at your next travel destination.

Inside this travel guide book you will find:

Visitor information from a Local
Tour ideas and inspiration
  Valuable guidebook information

Greater Than a Tourist- A Travel Guidebook with 50 Travel Tips from a Local. Slow down, stay in one place, and get to know the people and culture. By the time you finish this book, you will be eager and prepared to travel to your next destination.

OUR STORY

Traveling is a passion of the Greater than a Tourist book series creator. Lisa studied abroad in college, and for their honeymoon Lisa and her husband toured Europe. During her travels to Malta, an older man tried to give her some advice based on his own experience living on the island since he was a young boy. She was not sure if she should talk to the stranger but was interested in his advice. When traveling to some places she was wary to talk to locals because she was afraid that they weren't being genuine. Through her travels, Lisa learned how much locals had to share with tourists. Lisa created the Greater Than a Tourist book series to help connect people with locals. A topic that locals are very passionate about sharing.

TABLE OF CONTENTS

VISIT HISTORIC SITES, QUAYS, AND HARBOURS!

IMMERSE YOURSELF IN UNFORGETTABLE FUN ACTIVITIES

14. Stingray City and Snorkel Excursion

15. Rainforest Zip Lines

16. Antigua Reef Riders

17. Segway tour

18. Scuba diving and snorkeling

19. Kite Surfing

Sailing

20. Learn to Sail and Sailing Week

EAT OUT FROM LOCAL EATERIES TO FINE CUISINE.

21. Sweet T's

22. OJ's Beach Bar and Restaurant

23. Bar-Bs Restaurant and Bumpkins Beach Bar & Restaurant

24. Bay House Restaurant and Bar

25. Cecilia's High Point Cafe

26. Miracles of the Caribbean Restaurant and Bar.

27. Casa Roots Restaurant

28. Beach Limerz

TOP REASONS TO BOOK THIS TRIP

Packing and Planning Tips

Travel Questions

Travel Bucket List

NOTES

DEDICATION

This book is dedicated to my husband Nigel and children Marissa, Mikell and Malia, who have travelled with me.

ABOUT THE AUTHOR

Dr Edmondson is an Associate Professor at the American University of Antigua. She lives in Antigua and Barbuda with her husband and three kids and their pet cat Gabby. Gabby was a campus cat who was taken into their loving home.

Our Adorable Gabby □

Dr Edmondson loves singing and exploring the island and has a passion for dinghy sailing! She loves to cook and eat new foods. One of her island favorites is douchana and saltfish!

Dr Edmondson loves to travel, her family moved to Antigua and Barbuda 5 years ago. They love the gorgeous twin island that boasts 365 beaches!

To follow more of Dr Edmondson's travels, you can follow her on google maps where she is a google local guide with almost 1 million views of her photos!

https://www.google.com/maps/contrib/105798147 441532107047/photos/@17.0849644,- 61.8478904,12z/data=!3m1!4b1!4m3!8m2!3m1!1e1? hl=en-US

HOW TO USE THIS BOOK

The *Greater Than a Tourist* book series was written by someone who has lived in an area for over three months. The goal of this book is to help travelers either dream or experience different locations by providing opinions from a local. The author has made suggestions based on their own experiences. Please check before traveling to the area in case the suggested places are unavailable.

Travel Advisories: As a first step in planning any trip abroad, check the Travel Advisories for your intended destination.
https://travel.state.gov/content/travel/en/traveladvisories/traveladvisories.html

FROM THE PUBLISHER

Traveling can be one of the most important parts of a person's life. The anticipation and memories that you have are some of the best. As a publisher of the Greater Than a Tourist, as well as the popular *50 Things to Know* book series, we strive to help you learn about new places, spark your imagination, and inspire you. Wherever you are and whatever you do I wish you safe, fun, and inspiring travel.

Lisa Rusczyk Ed. D.
CZYK Publishing

WELCOME TO
> TOURIST

.

"Man cannot discover new oceans unless he has the courage to lose sight of the shore"

– Andre Gide

Antigua and Barbuda, is a twin island paradise where many tourists visit every year to experience the delight of the sparkling white sandy beaches and turquoise sea. Travelers enjoy the local cuisine warm sun and hospitality of the islands people.

Hop on a plane or sail the open ocean to experience this island paradise!

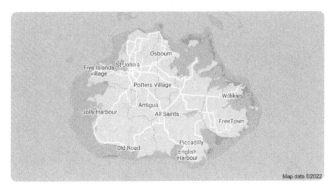

Antigua
Antigua and Barbuda

Antigua is an island in the lesser Antilles of the Caribbean region and is the main island of the country of Antigua and Barbuda. The name Waladli or Wadadli comes from the indigenous inhabitants for Antigua. The island is approximately 87 km (54 mi) by perimeter and the area is 281 km^2 (108 sq mi). The capital city is called *St. John's*.

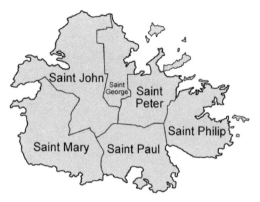

The map above shows the six parishes of Antigua.

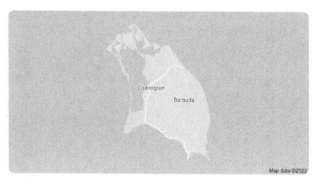

Barbuda
Antigua and Barbuda

Barbuda is located on the north of the island of Antigua. The total land is 160.56 km² (62 sq mi). The largest city is called *Codrington*, which has most of the inhabitants.

Antigua and Barbuda Climate

	High	Low
January	83	72
February	83	72
March	84	72
April	85	73
May	86	76
June	87	77
July	88	77
August	88	77
September	88	76
October	87	76
November	86	75
December	84	73

GreaterThanaTourist.com

Temperatures are in Fahrenheit degrees.
Source: NOAA

VISIT HISTORIC SITES, QUAYS, AND HARBOURS!

1. SHIRLEY HEIGHTS LOOKOUT POINT

This a historic site named after, Sir Thomas Shirley, Governor of the Leeward Islands, has one of the best views in Antigua. It stands approximately 490 ft above the ground, and you get the breathtaking view of English and Falmouth Harbours! The restaurant and bar and its famous Sunday evening party is always a hit.

The sunset sets are gorgeous and filled with iridescent colours. People enjoy birthdays, weddings, and anniversaries from this spectacular site.

This location is also a perfect spot for viewing the boats in Antigua's Annual Sailing week.

There is also the Lookout trail which runs from Galleon Beach to Shirley Heights. Galleon beach is a gorgeous beach with crystal clear waters, it would be worth the challenge to get there by trail. If, however, you want to drive from Shirley Heights to Galleon Beach that is a scenic short drive to that beautiful relaxing spot!

After a hike with the Antigua and Barbuda Brownies and Girl Guides, we were rewarded with this spectacular view! A perfect fusion of beautiful blue skies, cotton like cumulus clouds, the glory of the land, yachts moving gently in the wind and the white sandy beach!

I noticed that this beautiful cactus is often used an adornment in many gardens throughout the landscape.

2. PILLAR'S OF HERCULES

The staggering beautiful natural formation, the Pillars of Hercules, is a marvel to behold. It is formed by erosion of limestone rocks over many years. To get there you can continue your hike along Galleon Beach. Sea sprays often adds to the adventure.

An excursion with a group of medical students along Galleon beach to the Pillar's of Hercules was worth the view. It is mind-blowing that this is a natural rock formation when you are standing next to the pillars in all its glory!

Limestone Fact: Limestone is a sedimentary rock. It is composed of calcium carbonate (calcite) or a double carbonate of calcium and magnesium (dolomite). The northeastern part of Antigua 110 cm2 or 40% of the island is underlain with limestone. Limestone on the island is used for road building and construction.

Getting a rock wedgy is a cheeky pic ☺

Here is a view of the Pillar of Hercules from a Waddali Cat island Tours catamaran. It looks wonderful from the distance, but the appreciation the mighty rock formation is so much better up close!

A hiking detour behind the pillars of Hercules can take you further up to the mermaid pool/basin. Natural rock formation forms shallow pools which collect water, and it is wonderful to soak inside. To add to the novelty, bring along a mermaid tail and take a pic in the pool!

My little mermaid enjoying a soak in the mermaid pool ☺

3. NELSON'S DOCKYARD NATIONAL PARK

This park is a UNESCO world heritage site named after the British Hero of Trafalgar, Horatio Nelson, who served as the captain of the H.M.S Boreas. It is a unique naval site used from 1725 by the British Crown for the use of the Ships of war. It is the only Georgian dockyard in the world.

Today you can dine at their restaurants, eat from their bakery, and visit their museum. It is just amazing to experience that piece of history. An old sundial that is still there and spot on ontime!

The welcome board gives you key areas to visit.

That is some large anchor.

The faithful sundial still telling the time. It is reminiscent of childhood sundial assignments to tell the time.

In the Nelson Dockyard Museum, feel free to take all the silly pics with cutouts of British soldiers!

4. DOW'S HILL INTERPRETATION CENTRE

Near Shirley Heights the **Dow's Hill interpretation Centre** sits above English Harbour gives the best panoramic view of Nelson's Dockyard National Park. the panoramic view takes in the dramatic natural beauty of the park.

Dow's Hill was fortified in were in 1789 from a land attack. The fortification included Archibald Dow's house at the summit of the hill. Archibald Dow, the Dockyard Storekeeper, resided in the summit of the hill. When Royal Engineers appropriated his land in 1771, Mr. Dow received £8,354.0.8 compensation and the fortification was named after him.

Today the **Dow's Hill interpretation Centre** hosts multimedia presentation of Antigua and Barbuda's history.

Well preserved architectural history on top of Dow's hill.

The view of the ocean with perfectly placed seats to relax. It is so windy up there; you have to hold on to your hats and dresses or skirts!

At the interpretation centre on display a variety of shells.

5. ENGLISH HABOUR

English Harbour was developed as a British Navy base and served as the headquarters of the fleet of the Leeward Islands during the late 18th century.

Clarence House, a residence built for the future King William IV (1765-1837) overlooks English Harbour. *Shirley Heights* also overlooks English Habour.

6. DEVIL'S BRIDGE NATIONAL PARK.

This is located outside the village of Willikies. It is a stunningly gorgeous limestone rock which got its rugged good looks from millions of years of reef formation and erosion. This natural bridge has geysers and blow holes, so you must be careful where you stand.

The place where limestone, meets the raging sea and the blue sky.

Why is it called Devil's bridge? History has it that enslaved Africans would go there to commit suicide to escape the horrors of slavery. This led to the name Devil's bridge because of the numerous suicides.

Nowadays, this national historic site can be visited year long. One of the spectacles to behold is the annual kite flying events where hundreds of beautiful kites are hoisted.

The wind is perfect for hoisting these large inflatable kites. Hold on to your hats it is super windy here!

Finding Nemo is not hard to find if he is a giant inflatable kite!
Some of these kites require ten persons to hoist and maneuver them.

Can you spot the national flag of Antigua and Barbuda?

Hint: It has the colours black, blue, red, white and a golden sun. ☺

Black: symbolizes the soil and the people of African ancestry

Blue: means hope

Red: For the lifeblood of the slave forefathers and dynamism of the people.

White: means the Sun, Sand and Sea!

Golden Sun: symbolizes the dawn of a new era.

V: means victory at last!

7. OLD SUGAR MILLS AND THE RUINS OF BETTY'S HOPE.

As you drive around the island you will notice ruins or partially restored sugar mill towers. There are around 112 of them, not hard to miss! They serve as reminders of the brutal slave driven sugar industry of Antigua.

Betty's Hope is a former sugarcane plantation from the 17th century during British colonization. The sugar mill has undergone restoration, and the cotton house store has been transformed into a Visitor's Center.

8. VISIT THE MUSEUM OF ANTIGUA AND BARBUDA

The Antigua and Barbuda Museum is located in the capital of St John. It was opened the St. John Court House of 1750. In 1985, it opened to the public as a museum which gives visitors some of the island's history. You will see many artifacts from slavery and from the Amerindians. At the side of the building there is even an old red train.

9. HERITAGE QUAY

The Quay is the perfect spot to experience the bustle of St John. Many cruise ship passengers wander among the shops for the perfect souvenir. Locals and tourists enjoy the atmosphere of the waterfront promenade.

Many of the hundred-year-old buildings are maintained in their original form and adds to the quaint experience.

Cruise Ship docked and tourist embark on a discovery of the island.

Visitors can explore the numerous stores in the quay. The shopping is Duty-free with proof that their status is that of a traveler. Shoppers can take home colourful tropical clothing, the local arts and crafts. They can also purchase exquisite jewelry, Rolex watches, designer sunglasses and more.

Locals also dine out at the numerous restaurants and take in the vibrance of the atmosphere. Some dream of the day that they too will hop on a cruise!

10. ANTIGUA'S DONKEY SANCTUARY

This sanctuary is managed by the Antigua and Barbuda Humane Society. It is home to over 150 donkeys who were at risk. It is a joy to pet, brush, and play with the donkeys. Visitors can make donations or purchase memorabilia to help in support of this wonderful initiative.

11. MOUNT OBAMA

Named after the 44th President of the United States, Barack Obama. It was formerly known as Boggy Peak. It is the highest point in the southern Antigua Shekerley Mountain range at approximately 1300 feet. I hiked from a trail to get to the summit. The view was spectacular!

Mount Obama beckons me every time I look at this photo! I want to be a part of the scenery again rather than reminiscing the hike. With hikes, it is always important to wear comfortable shoes. Have adequate fluids to keep you well hydrated. Keep in the group that feels like they have your pace. As you ascend the summit, take lots and lots of pics!

12. JOLLY HARBOUR

Jolly Harbour is a resort style village located on the west coast of Antigua. You can choose to rent a condo for long or short term and enjoy the exotic surroundings many of the facilities and activities it has to offer. The Jolly Harbour Marina has mini-shops, restaurants, supermarket and gift shops. A sports centre keeps you quite active in their tennis and squash courts as well as their swimming pool. For the golfers it has an 18-hole championship course.

An amazing backdrop of the north finger of Jolly Harbour is a natural hill formation that looks like a sleeping woman, called the Sleeping Indian. In the south finger the Jolly Harbour beach is stretching out a mile long with white powdery sand.

From the villas in Jolly Harbour you get to see beautiful sunsets. No day is the same of course. This particular day was fascinating to me to see an orange hue in the sky superimposed by a perfect rainbow!

On Jolly Beach one Christmas time. Meet Sandy man. Making him was quite challenging, not as easy like snow. Getting the right amount of water in the sand

to make it compact does help a lot. It was all about portioning and trial and error when we did it.

Just bring along some coals, get some nearby sticks, conifer cones, add a carrot and a Santa hat and voila, you have got a Sandy Man!

He has an added advantage; he will never melt in the sun!

The joy on the face of this little mermaid on a rock says it all that it is fun to be outside in the sun on Jolly Beach!

13. FORT BARRINGTON NATIONAL PARK

This park was named after Admiral Barrington who fortified the fort in 1779. The fort was built to guard St. John's Harbour. It is a brief climb to reach the fort and you can see St John Habour, Deep Bay and the Royalton Hotel and the sea.

The climb to the summit of the fort can leave you breathless. You do not have to rush, just take a breather like my son before you venture on again!

*Once at the top of Fort Barrington, this gorgeous
view awaits you! Nature's beauty to behold!
A couple exchanged wedding views the first time I
was there. The next time there was a baptism and a
deliverance of the soul being conducted.
Whatever rocks your boat! It is definitely a place
that makes you feel divinity all around and inspires you
to do lifechanging things!*

View from Fort Barrington from another angle. Isn't this an extraordinary sight!
Deep Bay beach with the majestic Royalton Hotel can be seen at its end. The waters at this Deep Bay beach are very calm and clear. It is great for kayaking, snorkeling and picnics with friends!

IMMERSE YOURSELF IN UNFORGETTABLE FUN ACTIVITIES

14. STINGRAY CITY AND SNORKEL EXCURSION

This is a unique experience. You will be able to swim or snorkel with stingrays that are accustomed to human presence. They live freely and are not fenced. My family was able to feed them which was quite a thrill. It is safe for the whole family including children swimming besides them. You can take your own photos or allow the wonderful tour guides to have it professionally done, which can be printed before you leave or can be sent digitally to you. There is a sting ray shop where cute memorabilia can be bought. We still have a plush stingray and a key ring.

The dark halos are the stingrays on out in the ocean.
This particular spot is a sandbank, so you can stand
and see the stingrays or snorkel with them. I can still
recall the soft slipperiness of them when they swam by
me. At first, I thought it was scary, but overcame my
nerves and stayed calm to see these gentle animals.

I learnt that stingrays are fish, I never quite
classified them in a previous animal kingdom in my
mind, prior to this excursion.

I will have to revisit Stingray City again to get a
close-up photograph of these beautiful creatures. I
carefully put away my previous close-up photo and now

it cannot be found! It is now in a time capsule in some random place in the house ☺

Some Stingray vs Manta ray facts:
The stingray's mouth is found on the underside of its body.

The manta ray's mouth is found at the front edge.

Stingrays have eyes on the top of their body, whereas the manta rays have their eyes on the sides of their head.

Most stingray species possess a barb at the base of their tails.

Manta rays do not have barbs.

This begs the question are the stingrays in the Stingray city known to attack humans. These stingrays are acclimatized to human visits and are raised knowing humans and are fed by humans and have been quite gentle.

15. RAINFOREST ZIP LINES

This is an experience to get the adrenaline pumping as you zip through the canopy of Antigua's rich and lush rainforest. The Antigua Canopy Tour boosts that their youngest participant was 4 and oldest 99 years to date. Safety is number one and you are harnessed with state-of-the-art equipment and attended by qualified rangers.

Be sure to try this and receive your certificate of bravery upon completion of the tour!

16. ANTIGUA REEF RIDERS

This is an amazing water sport that takes you on turquoise water adventures. You get to sit and ride on an inflatable Reef Rider boat and go to selected secluded locations on Antigua's coast.

This adventure is coupled with a snorkeling session at Antigua National Marine Park. You can enjoy the stunning scenery by snorkeling at Cade's reef, which is a natural coral reef with gorgeous marine life. You can see lobsters, eels, parrotfish, rays, conch and more.

17. SEGWAY TOUR

Segway tour is a fun way to explore the island, especially if you want to see more without walking. On Segway you can explore the national landmarks, forts, museums, beaches and more. Popular beach tours are on Fort James and Runway beach.

18. SCUBA DIVING AND SNORKELING

Scuba diving in the clear and tranquil waters is breathtaking. Diving at Cades Reef, at different sites for sunken ships is always mind-blowing. You can choose to do a single dive experience or take a PADI course to be a certified diver.

The kids and a group of tourists snorkeling just off Green Island. This trip was part of a circumnavigation package with Waddali Cats Tours. The view was so mesmerizing, seeing the sea life is never tiring and ranges from exciting to tranquil.

19. KITE SURFING

This is one of the fastest growing water sports today. Kite surfing lessons can be done in Jabberwock on Judges' Bay. Beginners to advanced kite surfers can all enjoy this wonderful sport. Feel the freedom as the wind lifts you off the waters and floats you through the air.

SAILING

20. LEARN TO SAIL AND SAILING WEEK

The National Sailing Academy (NSA) in Falmouth Harbour offers free sailing to Antiguan school children. You can book activities like dinghy sailing, kayaking, paddle boarding or more just as a part of a one-time experience.

If you are staying a bit longer, you can enroll in the Royal Yachting Academy dinghy certification courses. Their trained instructor can take you sailing on a dinghy and teach you the ropes, literally!

Most recently the NSA launched their women on water activity and hoisted Antigua's first women only regatta on May 30th, 2022.

So, if you are coming for a vacation and would like to try something new or if you live on island and feel that your life is in a groundhog's day loop of work then home. Then you can try dinghy sailing.

The sailing instructors are amazing, they will sail you through the process of tacking, gybing and to watch out for that boom!

The takeoff from land to water feels like your cares have drifted away as you switch your thoughts onto something new. There will be a joyful dopamine rush with this sailing adventure!

Sailing Week

Antigua Sailing Week is a misnomer since it actually lasts for approximately a month in April. The sailing regatta is a highlight for yachties. Every year different events are held to enrich the event. You can get a great view of the event from Shirley heights. Lots of eat and drinking takes place at this venue. If you want a closer feel of the event you can join "Chase the race" on catamaran to get the best vantage point.

EAT OUT FROM LOCAL EATERIES TO FINE CUISINE.

21. SWEET T'S

You can at stop for a quick bite at Sweet T. They have quick a variety of local foods in an outdoor and airy environment. There is a playground for kids so that parents can relax. The ice-cream and desserts are amazing. Karaoke Sundays are fun when you want to belt out your own key!

The ice-cream parlor here has a range of delicious ice cream and sorbet. It is a delicious way to cool down anytime of day. One of the best times to cool down is after sailing at the National Sailing Academy. It is a treat on the ride from English Harbour back to St John's. **Can you spot the humongous whale bone in the pic?**

22. OJ'S BEACH BAR AND RESTAURANT

I love this place situated on the sandy beachfront. The decor is that of the sea, with shells, driftwood, and fishing nets. The catch of the day was a delicious Mahi Mahi fish washed down with lime squash.

This delicious Mahi Mahi fish with tender veggies before it disappeared down the depths of the hungry belly of my teenager ☺.

Just outside OJ's Beach Bar and Restaurant you can let the kids have fun frolicking on the white soft sandy beach. On a clear day you can even spot Montserrat.

23. BAR–BS RESTAURANT AND BUMPKINS BEACH BAR & RESTAURANT

Bar-Bs

This is situated next to Antigua Yacht Club. The price is affordable, and the quantity of food brims the plate. I love their sweet potato fries. You can relax the merry makers, admire the mega yachts from and look at the little optimist boats sail out from the Antigua Yacht Club.

Bumpkins Beach Bar & Restaurant

At this restaurant you can take in the gorgeous view of Pigeon Point Beach and Falmouth Harbor. Sip on your pina colada and enjoy Bar-B-Q chicken with green salad and more. The Saturday night live band is adding to the fun you can experience on the beach.

24. BAY HOUSE RESTAURANT AND BAR

There are many places on the island to dine alfresco on the beach, but Bay House is above ground away from you getting sandy toes. You get to dine on a gorgeous terrace with the breathtaking view of Dickenson's Bay. The entrance is a beautiful garden with tropical flowers.

Fish tacos with potato wedges, if you are not fussy for veggies, it is worth it for your cheat days from salads. There was a crunch in every bite!

Grilled Chicken with all the veggies missing in the previous meal.

The choice is yours and the range is great.

The a-la-carte menus are filled with fresh local products.

25. CECILIA'S HIGH POINT CAFE

This café is located on the water's edge with amazing ocean views in the backdrop. You can sip a glass of wine and stroll along the soft sandy beach. It is tightly tucked away close to Dutchman's Bay.

26. MIRACLES OF THE CARIBBEAN RESTAURANT AND BAR.

You can find them just at the entrance of Jolly Harbour Village Resort. The service is impeccable and so is the food. Live entertainment can sometimes enrich the atmosphere.

If you are a lobster lover, then when lobster is in season there will be no shortage of delicious lobsters on the menu in restaurants through Antigua and Barbuda.

This lobster dish in this photo was extra special because that night you could buy one and get the other half price off!

Note on Lobster Season*: The months of May and June are restricted for the consumption of all Lobster species. It is the mating season for lobsters, and we need young ones to replenish the sea.*

Other than those two months, lobster will be there on the menu to satisfy the palate.

27. CASA ROOTS RESTAURANT

Nestled between the beach and a tranquil garden, in a romantic, elegantly casual and relaxing setting, Casa Roots is stunning gorgeous rich blend of French and West Indian cuisine. It is flanked by the soft white powdery sandy beach and the Casa Roots Garden. The cuisine is fabulous that calls you to return time and time again. It is a thrill to the senses and great for couples or hanging out with friends.

Fish tacos on the beach. This was a first try for me. I placed this order after raving reviews from a friend. This fish was so tender and scrumptious.

I am not into mussels, but this was reported by my colleague as one of the tastiest mussels she's had on the island.

Mussels are harvest fresh on island.
Trivia:
How would you classify mussels? They are:
A fish
A crustacean
A mollusc
A reptile

Answer: c. A mollusc. Mussels have two hinged shells that are elongated and asymmetrical compared to the more oval clams.

28. BEACH LIMERZ

Beachlimerz is a beach paradise. They are nestled between Fort James beach and the Antigua's Historic Fort James. It is rich with Caribbean cuisine, live music, and entertainment. The cocktails are creative for example the tri-coloured Bob Marley cocktail!

You can spend the entire day by having fun with paddle boarding, kayaking, and snorkeling.

This cocktail is a tropical mix of fruit that is so refreshing! Enjoying a wonderful evening with your spouse and/or your friends on the beachfront on a moonlight night is a wonderful way to unwind your week. Karaoke nights are also wonderful, it is a time to carry your own key!

BEACHES, BEACHES, AND MORE BEACHES!

There are 365 beautiful beaches to enjoy! I am featuring the few that I frequent. But they all have their own beauty and grandeur.

29. FORT JAMES BEACH

It got its name from Fort James which is the fort of the entrance to St John's Harbour. It was built by the British to guard this harbour from possible French invasion in the 18th century.

This beach is located at Fort Bay on the northwest coast of Antigua. It is one kilometre of soft white sand. It is popular with cruise ship visitors and locals alike.

People relax under palm trees or sea grape trees. A good game of beach volleyball is often played.

Fort James Beach in her calm glory. This beach is not always calm, the waves can be rough. But on a good day, an inflatable kayak with a bunch of paddling kids makes for a fun-filled weekend.

30. PIGEON POINT

Pigeon's Point beach is in the southeast coast of Antigua and is located about a 5-minutes' drive from English Harbour. It is the closest beach to Falmouth Harbour and it's absolutely beautiful. You can enjoy jet skiing, sailing a dinghy or just soak in the crystal blue waters.

31. DARKWOOD BEACH

Darkwood beach is a long sandy beach on the southwest coast of Antigua, 15 miles from the capital of St. John's. It has gorgeous white beaches with iridescent seas. On a clear day Montserrat and Guadeloupe may be seen. You can enjoy swimming, sunbathing and scuba diving!

On Darkwood beach you can find Swash waterpark. It is a very entertaining water park for an energetic family. You can swim, splash, and jump on the 28 obstacles they provide. It can be quite a workout if you are not too fit, but for kids it is never a problem! If you prefer you can sit relax in their floating pool and enjoy the scenery.

32. DICKENSON'S BEACH

This beach is located on the Northwestern coast of Antigua. It is a stunning beach with powdery white sands and is the most developed beach on the island. This beach has various hotels along it, including Sandals. There is even a Kontiki bar out in the water get on a boat and have fun hanging out.

Sitting on the beach getting lost in the scenery, or just closing your eyes and listening to the crashing of the waves and the blowing of the wind is mind therapy at it's best. A ragged mind can be renewed.

Once renewed, soaking up this solitude is a natural way to synthesize fresh new ideas and vitamin D at the same time. This is an inoculation of healing at its best.

Other wonderful beaches I visited at least once or plan to visit are:

Hermitage Bay, Long Bay, Half-moon Bay, Deep Bay, Galleon Bay Beach, Jolly Beach, Runaway Beach, Dickenson's Bay, Buccaneer Cove Beach. These are remarkable beaches you would surely enjoy.

SUPERMARKETS, PHARMACIES AND BOOKSTORE.

There are many mini supermarkets and pharmacies on island. The ones mentioned here are frequently a lot by everyone.

33. EPICUREAN FINE FOODS

Epicurean Fine Foods & Pharmacy is Antigua's largest and most extensive grocery store and pharmacy. As the name says the groceries are of fine quality with a huge variety with an international appeal. You can also choose to take-out hot and freshly prepared meals. I am a fan of the Asian station. At the Asian station, you can have a variety of sushi, lowmein, sweet and sour chicken and fried rice for days you don't want to cook for yourself!

34. WOODS PHARMACY

They offer a wide variety of prescription and over the counter drugs. In addition, they sell cosmetics, household items, kid's gifts, greeting cards and more.

We also carry the complete range of cosmetics, gifts and household items.

35. CRAB HOLE LIQUORS & SUPERMARKET

Crab Hole Liquors and supermarket stocks a variety of grocery items, fresh local produce and as the name says liquors!

There is free delivery to Falmouth and English Harbor marinas.

36. ST. JOHN'S MARKET

Immerse yourself in the buzz of the Saturday morning market. You can enjoy a wide range of local fruits and vegetables. Some of these fruits are not usually found in the supermarkets for example finger rose bananas, chinip and more. A must have from the market is the Antigua Black Pineapple it is unique to the island.

There are souvenir and handcrafted items as well. If you want to start your own kitchen garden you can purchase the seedlings from the local vendors for e.g., lettuce, kale, corn, sweet peppers and many more.

If you like gardening, you can purchase seedlings at the public market area. Sometimes just a potted herbal garden may be all you need or if you want to try growing a vegetable garden then corn, cabbages, carrots, beets are all available for you to try.

At the public market you can find fruits like mammee apple, sapodilla, star apple, and grafted mangoes. They are all delicious and they each have their tropical richness to them.

These are sea grapes. The sea grape trees are abundant by the beaches, some even grow inland. I noticed that they grow very large and more abundantly by the beaches compared to inland trees. They have a sweetish, sour salty taste.

The nutritional value is thought to be the same as purple grapes and they are rich in copper, iron, potassium, and manganese.

Some people make jams or juices from them. I like eating them freshly picked or even pickled. If you never had one, it should be on your list to try!

BOOKS, BOOKS AND MORE BOOKS!

37. CINDY'S BOOK STORE

This bookstore is located in # 4 Townhouse Plaza, Corner American & All Saints Roads, Saint John's, Antigua. It hosts a large assortment
of textbooks and workbooks in all subjects for primary and secondary schools. In addition, kids can have educational toys, games as well as art & craft supplies.

38. BEST OF BOOKS.

The Best of Books is a general bookshop, a variety of books. The books range from children's books to romance novels, lining the main showroom. It has two levels and upstairs you can find cookbooks, religious, classics and inspirational books. For a small fee you can use their tables, chairs and computer and enjoy a good read. There is an upper reading room which is available for reading clubs, writer's clubs or by persons interested in foreign language classes or conducting writing workshops.

39. METHODIST BOOK SHOP

Methodist Book Shop is located in St. John's, Antigua and Barbuda. The sell schoolbooks, stationery, and art supplies as well. They specialize in selling many Christian books and many types of bibles. What make them unique is it has unique gift items, I still have a stove top Korean grill, talk about unique!

GIFTS AND DEPARTMENT STORES

40. TOWNHOUSE MEGASTORE

This is one of the finest department stores with a wide range of furniture, kitchen ware, electrical goods, garden furniture and toys. The service is fantastic Townhouse Megastore has something to suit all tastes and pockets & their sales service is first class.

41. SHOUL'S TOYS GIFTS & HOUSEWARES

The Shoul's Toys, Gifts & Housewares Store is Antigua's family store. It is located on the Newgate Street in St. John's City. Here you can get a wide range of items from toys, stationary, art supplies, party items, crockery, cutlery, bed and bath accessories. My favorite part about Shoul's is that they package gift items for every season, whether it is Christmas, Halloween, Valentine's, Easter and more.

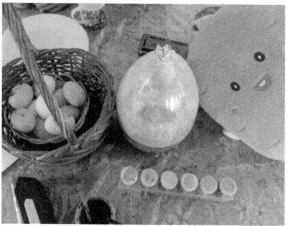

All these Easter supplies were from Shoul's Store, the Easter eggs with the paint in one package, a giant Easter egg to put treats, a stuffed plush carrot just because it is cute!

Our cat Gabby even got a water colour portrait of herself! When there is paint, creativity pours out!

42. COURTS FURNITURE STORE AND ASHLEY'S FURNITURE

Courts Furniture store is a Retail store that sells furniture, lighting equipment, electrical household appliances, and other household items. They are even selling electric motorbikes nowadays. They are suppliers of the state-of-the-art Ashley furniture. You can choose to pay in cash or in installments through hire purchase.

43. STOCK EXCHANGE

Shopping & Retail in Saint John's, Antigua and Barbuda

The Stock Exchange is a popular store for buying & selling top quality used items. If you want to relieve yourself of items, you don't need you can bring these items for Stock exchange to sell for you receive some bucks. Additionally, you can purchase wonderful items there as well. I got some gorgeous candle holders from this store.

CRICKET, CARNIVAL, AND CINEMA!

44. CRICKET

Whether you are a cricket fan or not you will have fun. You can follow the excitement of the game or have fun with the live entertainment and food at the event. It is amazing to see the Sir Vivian Richards cricket comes alive with an explosion of energy and people root on for their winning team!

Sir Vivian Richards is a retired Antiguan cricketer who is widely regarded as one of the greatest batsmen of all time.

For readers not sure what cricket is about, here it is summed up.

Cricket Summed up:

It is a bat and ball game which has two teams of eleven players each. At the centre of the cricket field is a 22-yard pitch with a wicket at each end. The aim of the game is to for the winning team to score the highest points without the batted ball being caught or hitting the wicket. This is a very overly simplified summary of it, as you learn the sport you can add the layers as the game is played.

Three fun cricket facts:

Cricket is the second most popular game in the world.

The longest ever cricket match lasted 12 days

Chris Gayle holds the record as the only batsman to hit a six from the first ball of a test match.

45. CARNIVAL

"Modern" Carnival Origins:

"Modern" carnival with all its feathered glory as we know it is believed to have originated fin Trinidad and Tobago in the late 18th century. Antigua celebrated its first carnival in August 1957. It is a celebration of emancipation from slavery.

Antigua's Carnival

Today, Antigua's Carnival continues to be an explosion of artistic and cultural talent. It serves a s tourist attraction as the streets of St John's and Carnival City at the Antigua Recreation Ground come alive with parades, Steel band music, calypso, and a multitude of masqueraders in colourful costumes.

It is a celebration of the emancipation of slavery in a ten-day festival.

The festivities range from the Panorama steel band competition, Party Monarch and Calypso Monarch and the Parade of Bands to the Miss Antigua Pageant and the Caribbean Queen's Competition.

This is sure to leave you with lasting memories of this cultural extravaganza.

Steelpan fact: *It is a percussion musical instrument that originated from Trinidad and Tobago.*

46. CARIBBEAN CINEMAS

Caribbean Cinemas Antigua, located in St John's, is part of a chain of movie theaters in the Caribbean. The theatre has 3D entertainment and a game arcade. Private screening and celebrations can be arranged.

Happy bunch of kids having movie-tastic -time, making awesome memories at a birthday party screening. There is something intrinsically special about going to the movie theatre and sharing that movie time together with friends!

My kids and friends having a fun time in the game arcade. Having fun in Game arcades is so much better than separate play on Roblox in separate homes! The social interaction is king!

47. LOCAL FOODS!

You will see BBQs with Johnny cakes or bakes across the island.

Ducana is made from sweet potatoes flavoured nutmeg & cinnamon. It can be eaten with saltfish.

Goat and Conch Water is also another island favourite.

Fungee and Pepper pot Antigua's national dish. Fungee is like a bread ball made from cornmeal. The pepper pot is a local cuisine with a bunch of meat and spinach.

FUNGEE RECIPE
(THE NATIONAL DISH OF
ANTIGUA AND BARBUDA).

Dry Ingredients:

2 cups of Cornmeal

1 tsp salt

6 Finely chopped okras

Wet ingredients:

4 cups water

1 tbsp butter or 1 tsp olive oil

Preparation:

Add water to the cornmeal until it is a wet paste.

Boil 4 cups of water and then add the okras and salt.

Turn in the wet cornmeal in the pot with a wooden spoon.

Lower the heat and allow to simmer for five minutes.

Stir the mixture to prevent lump formation.

Add more water if the mixture is too thick.

The fungee should be done in 20 to 30 minutes, careful not to burn it.

Butter or oil a small bowl. Place some of the fungee in the bowl and form a small ball and repeat the process.

Alternatively, you can butter or oil a small ramekin and place the fungee inside and gently remove from the ramekin and now your fungee will have the shape of the ramekin.

DUCANA RECIPE

Dry Ingredients:

1 ½ cups flour

Wet Ingredients:

2 cups grated coconuts or coconut flakes

2 cups grated sweet potatoes

1 ½ cups water

Optional: grated carrots.

Spices:

1 tsp cinnamon

1 tsp ground nutmeg

1 tbsp vanilla extract

Optional: 1 cup raisins

Banana leaves and kitchen twine or foil

Preparation:

1.Mix all the wet ingredients together except the water.

2. Add flour to form a cohesive dough. Add water if the dough is too dry.

3. Cut the washed banana leaves into 6-to-12-inch squares. Heating the banana leaves into gentle fire can make them more pliable.

4. Place some of the dough in the centre of the banana leaf. Wrap the dumplings in banana leaves and use aluminum foil or twine for reinforcement. Repeat until all your dough is finished.

5. Boil the banana wrapped dough for 30 to 45 minutes. It is softer or firmer is left for 30 or 45 minutes. Ensure the bubbles are not too violent, it must be a gentle boil.

6. Remove and leave on a cooling rack.
   Your ducana will be ready to eat when cooled!

   Fruits like mangoes and chinip when in season are sweet and delicious!

   Mangoes are my favourite food! Indulge me in my poetic tribute below to this delicious, flavourful and mouth-watering fruit the Mango!

Mangoes! Mangoes oh beautiful, yummy mangoes!
It is so abundant, everywhere it grows!
Mangoes make me sing,
Mangoes make me walk with a swing.
How could there be such a magical thing.
This fruit is a tropical king.
It could be mango season all year long and I won't
mind at all.
As long as I am eating it, I will be having a ball!

BARBUDA

This is the sister island to the twin island nation. Most of the residents live in the *town of Codrington.* It is famed for the *pink sand beach, caves, and the frigate bird sanctuary.*

The pink sand beach is known to be the pinkest in the Caribbean region.

Why is it pink? This is due to the high levels of corals along the coast. The sand has a champagne colour due to crushed coral in the mix of the white sand.

How can you get to Barbuda? You can get there by a 90-minutes ferry ride or by air to the Barbuda Codrington Airport.

48. BARBUDA CAVES

Barbuda is a limestone island that has several caves that adventure seekers would love to explore.

Darby Dave's huge sinkhole and is located three and a half miles northeast of Codrington Village. The sinkhole is over 300 feet in diameter and about 70ft deep. There are 8ft long stalactites on one side of the cave.

Two Foot Bay is a cave that winds its way underground for about a mile. It has ancient petroglyphs carved by Arawak Indians. This can be seen among the stalagmites and stalactites.

The Dark Cave has rare amphipods, blind shrimp and many bat species!

49. VISIT THE FRIGATE BIRD SANCTUARY

This sanctuary is massive where more than five thousand frigate birds reside around the swamps and mangroves. It is the largest of its kind in the western region. It is a bird watcher's paradise, these nagnificent birds travel between the Caribbean and Galapagos islands during the mating seasons. The lagoon can only be accessed by licensed sea taxi from the Codrington jetty. The most popular time to visit is during the mating season, from September to April (December is peak time). It is mesmerizing to see the blood-red inflating throat pouches of these amazing birds.

FLY HIGH AND SEE IT ALL!

50. CALVIN AIR HELICOPTER TOUR

The helicopter tour is absolutely fantastic. You get to travel in a state of the art fully air-conditioned helicopter to soak in the panoramic view of Antigua and Barbuda. These memories are bound to leave an indelible make on your memory. Not only do you get tours of Antigua and Barbuda, but the Monsterrat Volcano Tour and the Heaven and Earth Experience, the latter of which combines land and air tours. It was mind blowing to see the coral reef from above and see turtles and they swam in the turquoise waters.

Calvin Air's Helicopter. This flying steel machine is a multimillion-dollar marvel. It has comfort in mind by

being airconditioned and it gives a spectacular panoramic view. The pilot commented that he never had so many curious questions on a tour prior to our trip, lol. The excitement and amazement were too much to contain, it stimulated a slew of what is this and where is that and lots of oohs and aahs!

A bird's eye view from Calvin Air's helicopter. A salt pond separated by a beachy sand bank from the open blue ocean. Yachties pepper the ocean with boats, and they take in the gorgeous natural beauty.

A view of nearby British territory, Montserrat's Soufriere Hills volcano. The sleeping behemoth became active in 1995, destroying the capital city of Plymouth. You can see where the pyroclastic activities occurred from the side of the Soufriere Hills.

Thankfully no major threat to Antigua. People on the west side of Antigua sometimes say they can smell the Sulphur blowing over from Montserrat from time to time.

TOP REASONS TO BOOK THIS TRIP

Beaches: There are 365 beaches to explore!

Food: The amazing food!

Island Culture: Rich cultural experience!

Beaches and white sand are everywhere for fun filled moments for these young friends. This location is at the Siboney beach front, a stone's throw away from the Sandal's Grande beach front on Dickenson's Bay.

Burying a friend in the sand never gets old, followed by a huge splash in the blue sea to wash that sand off!

DID YOU KNOW?

Did you know that **Antigua and Barbuda is Spanish for 'ancient' and Barbuda is Spanish for 'bearded'**?

Did you know that Antigua was also known as **Waladli or Wadadli** by the native population which is an Arawak word meaning **"our own"**?

Did you know that **Warri** is a board game popular in Antigua which traces its origins back to Africa?

There is so much joy when a child can run on the water's edge, feel the wet sand under her toes, the waves caressing the little feet and being sun kissed and cooled by the Caribbean breeze! This is island life!

ANTIGUAN AND BARBUDAN DIALECT

It is an English-based language formed by slaves as they imitated their slavers and used their own pronunciation.

Here are a few that you can familiarize yourself with!

English:Hot
Dialect: Hat
Use in a sentence: The sun is hat hat!

English: Trouble
Dialect: Chubble.
Use in a sentence: That boy is chubble!

English: I don't like it
Dialect: Me nah like um.

English: cucumber
Dialect: qucumba
Combined with the above dialect: Me nah like qucumba.

English: Me nah go deh
Dialect: I am not going there.

English: No, not me or not at all
Dialect: Tall or tarl
Combined with the above dialect: Me nah go deh tarl!
Meaning: I am not going there at all!

Antiguan slang: "you hear ah knuckle he get knuckle?!"
English: "Did you hear that his girlfriend cheated on him?!"

NATIONAL SYMBOLS

The National Flag

We spoke about the national flag early. It a national symbol and was designed by Mr. Reginald Samuel in 1966.

The National Bird

We also spoke of the Frigate bird, *Fregata magnificen,* it is the national bird of Antigua and Barbuda.

The National Sea Creature

It is the Hawksbill turtle (Eretmochelys imbricata). It is on the endangered list.

The National Fruit

The Antiguan Black Pineapple (*Ananas comosus*) is mainly grown on the south side of Antigua. It was originally introduced by the Arawaks, and was used for making twine, cloth and for healing purposes.

The National Tree

The Whitewood (*Bucida buceras*) is a wide-spreading ornamental shade tree. It is related to the mangroves and almond trees. It was once used for making gun carriages due to its heavy and hard timber.

The National Animal

It is the European Fallow (*Dama dama dama*) deer. They live and breed in only in Barbuda and Guiana Island and do not live in any other Eastern Caribbean Island. There are two varieties black and common.

The National Flower

The Dagger Log's (*Agave karatto Miller*) produces yellow flowers which rises from the Agave plant. The flower's log (or stem) used to be used for making fishing rafts and fishing bait was made from the white interior pulp of the leaves.

The National Dress

The madras textile is worn proudly by Antiguans and Barbudans on the National Day.

The National Stone

It is called the petrified wood. This is fossilized wood which was buried in volcanic ash for extended periods of time. This found may still be found scattered throughout central Antigua.

Coat of Arms and Motto
"EACH ENDEAVOURING, ALL ACHIEVING"
is the motto of Antigua and Barbuda. It was
composed by Mr. James H. Carrot M.B.E.

The coat of arms has many of the national symbols
depicted on it as well as unique landmarks. These
include the Antigua Black Pineapple, the red hibiscus,
the golden sun, wavy blue and white bands for the
sun and sea, the sugar mill tower and stem of sugar
symbolic of the former sugar industry, the dagger log
plant with a pole and golden yellow flowers, the
European Fallow deer that is endemic to Antigua and
Barbuda and finally the scroll with the motto of the
nation.

Rescue a Pet
*Having rescued my pet, Gabby, it has added much
happiness to my family's life. I must say thanks to
Brianne Schwartz and Dr Dawn Roberts for cajoling
me into having her, a decision I do not regret!*

*Since then, I have encouraged others to rescue
pets. I feel that I have a civil duty to encourage others
to have a pet, they do bring a lot of joy in our homes.
Pets need us just as much as we need them!*

Please see below info on PAAWS Antigua.

PAAWS Antigua:

Protect Antiguan Animals With a Smile (PAAWS) was opened on March 8th, 1996, and is licensed by the Dog Registration and Control authority. They are associated with the RSPCA and is a member of the Caribbean Animal Welfare Group.

They are a non-profit animal shelter that rescue pets and they do a phenomenal job. Donors are asked to support their spay/neuter program, shelter maintenance, vet care, humane primary school education. Even a visit to the shelter is welcomed.

Whenever you are just in need of pressing your reset button, this could be you lying around rejuvenating, recharging, and reviving the lion in you!

ISLAND TRIVIA

1) What is the capital of Antigua and Barbuda?

2) What is then name of the international airport?

3) How long is Antigua?

4) How is the head of state?

5) What is the currency used in Antigua and Barbuda?

6) What do locals usually like to eat with BBQ?

7) What is the name of the private island paradise?

8) What is the former name of Mount Obama?

9) Name the hurricane that destroyed Barbuda in 2017.

10) What is the national fruit?

ANSWERS

1) St. John's
2) V.C. Bird International Airport
3) 14 miles long.
4) The British monarch.
5) The Eastern Caribbean dollar.
6) Johnny cakes
7) Jumby Bay Island
8) Boggy Peak
9) Irma
10) The black pineapple

PACKING AND PLANNING TIPS

A Week before Leaving

- Arrange for someone to take care of pets and water plants.

- Email and Print important Documents.

- Get Visa and vaccines if needed.

- Check for travel warnings.

- Stop mail and newspaper.

- Notify Credit Card companies where you are going.

- Passports and photo identification is up to date.

- Pay bills.

- Copy important items and download travel Apps.

- Start collecting small bills for tips.

- Have post office hold mail while you are away.

- Check weather for the week.

- Car inspected, oil is changed, and tires have the correct pressure.

- Check airline luggage restrictions.

- Download Apps needed for your trip.

Right Before Leaving

- Contact bank and credit cards to tell them your location.

- Clean out refrigerator.

- Empty garbage cans.

- Lock windows.

- Make sure you have the proper identification with you.

- Bring cash for tips.

- Remember travel documents.

- Lock door behind you.

- Remember wallet.

- Unplug items in house and pack chargers.

- Change your thermostat settings.

- Charge electronics, and prepare camera memory cards.

READ OTHER
GREATER THAN A TOURIST
BOOKS

> TOURIST

Follow us on Instagram for beautiful travel images:
http://Instagram.com/GreaterThanATourist

Follow *Greater Than a Tourist* on Amazon.

CZYKPublishing.com

METRIC CONVERSIONS

TEMPERATURE

110° F —	
100° F —	— 40° C
90° F —	— 30° C
80° F —	
70° F —	— 20° C
60° F —	
50° F —	— 10° C
40° F —	
32° F —	— 0° C
20° F —	
10° F —	— -10° C
0° F —	— -18° C
-10° F —	
-20° F —	— -30° C

To convert F to C:

Subtract 32, and then multiply by 5/9 or .5555.

To Convert C to F:

Multiply by 1.8 and then add 32.

32F = 0C

LIQUID VOLUME

To Convert:...................Multiply by
U.S. Gallons to Liters................ 3.8
U.S. Liters to Gallons 26
Imperial Gallons to U.S. Gallons 1.2
Imperial Gallons to Liters....... 4.55
Liters to Imperial Gallons 22
1 Liter = .26 U.S. Gallon
1 U.S. Gallon = 3.8 Liters

DISTANCE

To convert ....Multiply by
Inches to Centimeters 2.54
Centimeters to Inches 39
Feet to Meters...................... .3
Meters to Feet 3.28
Yards to Meters 91
Meters to Yards 1.09
Miles to Kilometers 1.61
Kilometers to Miles............ .62
1 Mile = 1.6 km
1 km = .62 Miles

WEIGHT

1 Ounce = .28 Grams
1 Pound = .4555 Kilograms
1 Gram = .04 Ounce
1 Kilogram = 2.2 Pounds

115

TRAVEL QUESTIONS

- Do you bring presents home to family or friends after a vacation?

- Do you get motion sick?

- Do you have a favorite billboard?

- Do you know what to do if there is a flat tire?

- Do you like a sun roof open?

- Do you like to eat in the car?

- Do you like to wear sun glasses in the car?

- Do you like toppings on your ice cream?

- Do you use public bathrooms?

- Did you bring a cell phone and does it have power?

- Do you have a form of identification with you?

- Have you ever been pulled over by a cop?

- Have you ever given money to a stranger on a road trip?

- Have you ever taken a road trip with animals?

- Have you ever gone on a vacation alone?

- Have you ever run out of gas?

- If you could move to any place in the world, where would it be?

- If you could travel anywhere in the world, where would you travel?

- If you could travel in any vehicle, which one would it be?

- If you had three things to wish for from a magic genie, what would they be?

- If you have a driver's license, how many times did it take you to pass the test?

- What are you the most afraid of on vacation?

- What do you want to get away from the most when you are on vacation?

- What foods smell bad to you?

- What item do you bring on ever trip with you away from home?

- What makes you sleepy?

- What song would you love to hear on the radio when you're cruising on the highway?

- What travel job would you want the least?

- What will you miss most while you are away from home?

- What is something you always wanted to try?

- What is the best road side attraction that you ever saw?

- What is the farthest distance you ever biked?

- What is the farthest distance you ever walked?

- What is the weirdest thing you needed to buy while on vacation?

- What is your favorite candy?

- What is your favorite color car?

- What is your favorite family vacation?

- What is your favorite food?

- What is your favorite gas station drink or food?

- What is your favorite license plate design?

- What is your favorite restaurant?

- What is your favorite smell?

- What is your favorite song?

- What is your favorite sound that nature makes?

- What is your favorite thing to bring home from a vacation?

- What is your favorite vacation with friends?

- What is your favorite way to relax?

- Where is the farthest place you ever traveled in a car?

- Where is the farthest place you ever went North, South, East and West?

- Where is your favorite place in the world?

- Who is your favorite singer?

- Who taught you how to drive?

- Who will you miss the most while you are away?

- Who if the first person you will contact when you get to your destination?

- Who brought you on your first vacation?

- Who likes to travel the most in your life?

- Would you rather be hot or cold?

- Would you rather drive above, below, or at the speed limited?

- Would you rather drive on a highway or a back road?

- Would you rather go on a train or a boat?

- Would you rather go to the beach or the woods?

TRAVEL BUCKET LIST

1.

2.

3.

4.

5.

6.

7.

8.

9.

10.

NOTES

Printed in Great Britain
by Amazon

14593298R00078